HOME OF MELANCHOLY

Barbara Maria Michalska

PublishAmerica
Baltimore

First printing

At the specific preference of the author, PublishAmerica allowed this work to remain exactly as the author intended, verbatim, without editorial input.

ISBN: 1-4137-8115-2
PUBLISHED BY PUBLISHAMERICA, LLLP
www.publishamerica.com
Baltimore

Printed in the United States of America

Home of Melancholy

To the editor
Rebecca Wigood
from
author

[signature]

In memory of Petronela and Wladyslaw Moroz

A map of life

Growing and receding pain runs feverishly across a map
Of
Mind

Like a river

Unable
To
Reverse
Once established course

Dreams postponed for any reason
Gain on importance with the passage
Of
Time

Taking on a role of inspiration in new attempts at
Hidden enclaves
Of life

By
Virtue
Of maintaining the source of its existence

Enhanced by continuous effort endeavours of a day
Stand out
In
A complacent ocean of mediocre preoccupations

Harbouring new hopes as they emerge every day from islands
Of
Endurance

A view of Island of Terra

Sun was gently pleasing my age
And I favoured time to be
An accessory

For
Larger than life events

When I walked away like a stranger
Never to be reminded

Of
A duty
To go back and give an account

Of
Undertaken tasks

As often is the case I navigated my life in servitude
Of
Unfavourable circumstances

Naïve at first of learning qualities of any given
Experience

Even though a desert already painted its ominous presence
Along my every effort

Leaving a disturbing site for pain self inflicted
By
Nomadic predisposition of memory

In a journal of my ill-conceived journey
I write daily

Yesterday I watched once again tropical slopes of Terra Nova
As they change on approach into vision of inhospitable cliff

A sudden feeling of dismay

All at once even eye-pleasing tree branches become nakedly
Prosaic

Birds chant the same longing song as if they were not capable
Of
Stopping
This prolonged sadness of monotony

I reach for a mirror finding no solace in tears traveling down
My
Cheek

Maybe they will leave a permanent shadow around my eyes
Or
Scar the surface of glass reflection

I perform well a task of hiding from others a feeling
Of
Dismay

Anchoring it to the depths of my heart weakened with bitterness

But when I am alone I go on my knees reaching out
To
Healing properties of earth

Ashes of my bones

I came back from ashes of my bones to watch the flow of river
Charging forth into my open veins

Sprouting branches of trees bend gracious necks
Above born again earth feeding hearts in need of beauty

Reality has many gates each one opening a mystery of life
To those who are willing to fill the gaps of destiny

Words of wisdom incepted at the time of trial lead us out
Of self imposed prison

Allowing for new images to proliferate from desolate landmarks
Of mind

I came back from ashes of my bones into the fold of welcoming
My return plain with a view at a horizon drawing borders

Not to be crossed again

Memory of the past

At times when moon wilfully strays away from
Its
Well-established path

Meadows blanketed by night play host to wild roses whispering
In
Dark

Reminiscing a high cliff near a shimmering creek where
They
Once stood without calling for attention

A prehistoric fish meanders on the bottom
Of
Dried out riverbed home

Calling me from behind curtains
Of
Ages

To resume search for graves of my ancestors who vanished
Before
They had a chance to leave behind
Monuments

To lean on messages from fables depicting human strife
Able
Of lifting sadness of heart
When unfulfilled promises become a burden

To learn from an exuberant bird taken by vastness of space

In
Its first solitary flight

Away from wilderness away from
Its nest

To be always vigilant knowing a man falls a prey to
Another man

Behind my closed eyes I see a parade of names

Of
Past heroes

Incrusted in calligraphy on ancient plates
Included in epistles

They fate embraced by life and death's unexpected turns

At the gate to a new millennium

Stars are permitted to see well beyond spectrum of lesser value
Miracles

Lost in ways of everyday life confused by ingenious names
Of new and distant centuries

You are back standing now at the gate to the next millennium
Measuring gains with a scale of price you have paid
For redemption
Of sin

Your wounds are heeled but scars still visible estrange sensibilities of many
Who find it too imposing on pride to acknowledge presence
Of
Son of God once condemned to death by a man

With finality unknown to mercy

You want to go to Egypt on retrospective
Journey

To see first hand places where faith had once persevered on sediments
Of
Nile River older than words in command over chaos

Desert will deliver you further still across the sea to an ancient city
Of
Jerusalem

Where stricken by sunshine walls are prophesying your homecoming
Breathing out nostalgic sentiment

Over the only tomb overgrown with climbing rosebushes

Autumn in a garden

Autumn delivers baskets filled with late blooming flowers
Freshly picked fruits

Regretfully at the request of night days become shorter
Morning chill spreads over distant ranges
Of
Hills on a lowering its eyelids horizon

Giving in to melancholic mood I dream a stranger
Visits me at home

He places corral necklace around my neck
Around my arm he skilfully arranges a scarf
In
All shades of gold

Wrapped in a veil of suspense we enter the gate
To a place where fate of leaves
Illuminated
By
The last evening rays has already
Been decided

By
Unyielding will of a season

A clock strikes midnight hour

I open my eyes to find myself alone holding the last bleeding leaf
A garden has fallen asleep

Average man

Average man devotes his time to cultivating
A piece of a chosen fallow

He is tending cabbage while listening to whispers
Of
Delicate flowers at the back of his courtyard

Planting seeds of trees along roads winding their tails
In an attempt to cut through

To
The other side of a horizon

Where
Crows escape from their predators

At dawn blue sky alighted with a new covenant
Makes him believe
The rules
Of
Land will always be upheld

On an approach of final limit his last effort completes
Its
Turn

He is at peace with himself when he is summoned
To gods

Be done with choruses

Find a will to write a poem explaining the explicit nature
Of
A horizon
Hiding the immense distances from human eyes

Converse with autumn when its leaves are falling down
To
Your feet rushing yet aimless

Be done with winter spring summer choruses
In
Time to make prolonged leisure of evenings

Remind me only if you believe love will once reveal its true meaning
In
A few unrelated incidents

Childhood memory

In my fondest memory I see a nest of stark family
On
A tall red chimney

Under eye eluding sky hanging low in autumn
I hear insatiable yearnings of a working sawmill

Overwhelmed with sensation I step on a thin ice over a small creek
In
A heart of village

Invisible in a mounting heat of summer I cross meadows frequented
By
Wild rabbits and elks

Desert love

You don't travel the expanse of desert with me anymore
But
Try not to relinquish every ritual

I'm on my route urged to move forward by day
At
Night returning to the well of waiting

A willing mouth of oasis deprives me not
Of
Greenery water or sleep

I walk miles before I succumb to an illusion
Of
A morning also in confusion

At noon devil rests its hand upon my forehead
In
A gesture of agreement

Pulsating blade of light blinded my searching eyes
Now
I became one of the sun's most dutiful daughters

Maybe you disdain craving for sensual giveaways known
To
Arid places

My need of love awakens near shallow breathing
Of
Dunes in a state of complete neglect

Escape

Desert route takes him out now escaping
All
Of his loud oppressors

Overcoming a storm of yellow wind Jesus
Finds half sunken gate

To
A valley of lilies
On the evening of the third day

Memory of recent events exploits his willingness
To
Endure far more than will be testified

In
Years to come
By his less hearted followers

Night will dispatch temporary measures
Of
Healing upon his wounds

In the first hour of dawn he will be called upon
To rise above wilderness

Feast at night

Through a veil of intuition I see you welcoming mirages
Of
Iconographic designs

Grandiose landscapes befit mind
Invited by forces of unknown to a residence
Of
Prolific visions feeding on hunger of young
And inexperienced

Mesmerized by constellations you think it is only human
To chase after distant planets

Their place in a higher order of universe elusive yet constant
Allows for a delusion of vast empire crying out into night

Beyond the familiar patterns of skies

You investigate darkness travelling light heartedly into carcases
Of eclipses broken by tails of comets into a wave of lightning

Not knowing if unfaithful angels are still on your side

Morning offers its saviour's hand limiting findings of night
To
A gamble of tangible colours

And you become overwhelmed at once by magnificent implications
Of your own being

Like a Fire Fox

Like a Fire Fox you know how to avoid danger hiding from uninvited visitors
Under the cover of trees extending a dark coat above your home

You roam a density of forest where sun is prevented from entering
Allowing for safety as you move swiftly from shadow to shadow

You announce your presence in a voice tuned with the sounds
Of never disclosing all its brewing secrets wilderness

Like a Fire Fox you make appearances in open fields to witness
The last longing breath of wind lingering over wet patches of marsh

Capable of prevailing against a sudden wave of storm you move fast towards
The unknown in search of the next trial to reassure your strength

Despite an intrusion of eyes eager to condemn your bearings you have courage
To declare rights to your own freedom

Like a Fire Fox you respect the resolves of always a step ahead from
Our understanding
Fate

A Fire Fox in you elevates your spirit above a tide of hardship renewing
Commitment to earth

Grass of Garden of Eden

Status quo arrangement with humankind
Expired its validity for
Fastidious
God

In his wisdom he will no longer deny
Indiscriminating nature
Of
Sin

Arriving at conflicting answers
To
His failure at the time of creation and to our
Misfortune

Deceived by poignant anger in dealing
With
Lawless roots of insubordination

He is not able to dismiss
Sombre aftermath
Of
Self imposed exile
From everyday prayers delivered
By
Vanity seeking man

Acknowledging his own deviation from rules

Of
Sound judgment

He practises humility equal
To
His very teachings
As he puts aside the Book of Genesis
In
A gesture of indecision

Meanwhile

Far from our eyesight grass of Garden of Eden
Is
Being kept meticulously green

Grass is silent

Grass is silent and I became its companion in silence
Where
Loneliness finds a niche
Away
From the pretence of languages

Until now someone was holding my hand
Either to fill me with courage
Or
Cater to own comfort of mind

But even an angel deserts a man to his
Fate

And a man becomes an angel himself
Disillusioned

Standing alone on a road to heavenly gate
Unable

To ask for early admittance

Because sun still answers many prayers sending a doze
Of light
In
Service to prolong
The miracle
Of

Another morning unfolding
A new promise

Upon the pride of earth
Where human dreams are not to be betrayed

Hermit

He is adept in solitude in return solitude guides him
To
Practice habits of perfection

He takes apart a fibre of ensuing question upon
Commonly accepted rules
Of
Ethics
And applies to them his own peripheral view of society

In strict adherence to self discipline
He
Allows
No weakness
Compromise his duty

Confined not by degree of wealth
But rigours of simplicity
He

Chooses to attend to his basic needs
Only

He unites with minds of his predecessors
In
Revering
Daily ritual of dawn

Hopeful for something

By a fountain I stop to give rest to my tired feet
Feeling that hope is rushing
To
My rescue

Light passes gently through waterfall changing
Its
Décor into vision of gold

Sunset prolongs its presence on a horizon
Fulfilling its obligation

I feel I travelled the path of solitaire to the very end

Deprived
Of
Words to supplement my feelings
I am free at last from requirements
Of
Reality

Sparks of rays follow the water flow
To
Life sustaining main artery of earth
The life-giving source

I test the softness of water with my hands
The last worry behind me

Still waiting for something to happen on this day
Something extraordinary

Unaware of His presence until I recognize the suffering in His eyes
From
Old oil paintings

If you wish

If you wish we could sit on a nearby meadow
Just you and
Me
Among noisy crows and fighting sparrows

If you wish we could start a debate
Just you and
Me
Over fallen leaf conclusion

If you wish we could follow seldom traveled road
Just you and
Me
Until speed becomes the only interference

White flowers of frenzy

White flowers of frenzy captivated my mind alone
In a hot summer evening

Putting aside initial misgivings I listened to a voice
Of an old destitute patriarch

Reciting passages from bible revised
By zealots of deception

To saw the seeds of a new religion

Led by a skillful demagogue of irrational I fell into belief
To gain a place of my own in the realm of a new
Utopia
Governed by gods who lost power of revenge

Defying sense of safety I strayed away far from protective hands
Of
Reality
Falling into carnival of night inhabited by phantoms
Pretending to be angels

But crafted into predicted pattern the return of dawn
With the ruling laws of season became imminent

I found my reason preserved at last at the end
Of
Writing its falsehood epic

As I listened to Viva Vitae!
Shouted
By
Early pedestrians

As seen in the eyes of sun

You were standing by the window watching night change into day
In a sudden surge
Of
A blaze

I did not see your eyes filtered with light by exposure
To sun

Blue-and-white angel told you in well-chosen words
Not
To step further than always craving for more emptiness
Spread behind green range of hills

It was summer of June that changed your appearance to
A sight
Of
A swift bird
With a gesture of all justifying finality

You were about to leave
The zone of safety attributed to an embrace of familiar scene

With a hesitant move forward you came to accept
The loss of earth chilly under
Your feet

In the meantime I knelt down by the gilded with ornaments
Gate
Leading back to mornings alighted with love

An invitation

Come to me before midnight when night sits quietly
Above horizon

Come to me at dawn hour when song
Of birds affirms our willingness

Come to me at noontime to witness wandering
Sun in its zenith

Come to me in the evening we will listen
To piano concertos

Love temptations

There is love invoked by always present glamour
Of
The sky

A blue enterprise escapist by its nature

There is love of flowers at the end of their season
When

They bend down gracefully exhibiting a full bloom
Unwilling
Yet

To
Fade away unnoticed

Prolonging their departure

There is love of playful snowman sought after

In
Time
Of great disappointments

There is a compassion for someone who falls into arms
Of love temptations

Sailor of the night

Craving the beauty of stars I am a sailor of night steering along
Unknown archipelagos

Silver blue seagulls break silence with a sound of warning
Accustomed only to a sight of friendly angels

In a distance a stream of fast moving cars hijacked by the will
Of carefree drivers speeds straight into the space precipice

Above a face of moon displaying its imprisoned smile navigates
A lantern like a lighthouse keeper veteran of solitude

A newly acquired feeling of freedom helps me manoeuvre with ease
Among emerging phantoms of atolls

My goal is to reach majestic group of icebergs where the last port
Is home to all voyagers

Medusa's sunset

Tomorrow I must resurface again blinded by oncoming tide
Each time seems to be the last

My strength afforded by a necklace a priest able to foresee all
Gave me at birth

It's inscribed with names of fish birds and seaweeds
Forced into contest of
Life

Hope is justly being hailed for a redeeming value transcending
Passing moments
Into

Mind feeding legends captured in a faltering prism of light
To deliver us from chains of misery

Any effort has its own way of knowing how to cross a fine line
Between caution gained with age and insatiable will
Of
Wonder unyielding to rules imposed

Aided with our perception acquired in moods of melancholy
We follow the sun descending upon skyline stooped above the earth

Until it slowly slides behind mountain crest or balances for a while
On its own last glimmer inviting torments of dusk

Premonition prevails not everything has been finalized to one's satisfaction
Perhaps forever lost unfulfilled omitted

Our hands remain still on guard at windowsills
We choose to fall into belief matters have been resolved
To the benefit of all
By
A Grand Master of stage

Yet we are unable to discern the fact that moon a dispassionate medium
Waits in a pool of silence behind the last curtain
Willing
To
Depict someone's worrisome face pretty soon

Home of melancholy

Rain stimulated by its alter ego falls down long
Into
Evening hours

I see a mist in front of an island carved out like a small toy
By
Its crafty design

You are trying to rescue me from unyielding cravings
Of
My need to travel to the other shore

Cater to my temporary absence of mind with fragile words
Only
Age has a permission to use

Lead me above steep walls all the way to the breathing space
Of
The highest cliff

And back to safety again

Until at last I find a place for treasure scattered upon the surface
Of
Earth in a true home of melancholy

Where roses are blooming every season with the same benevolent
Intention

Memento

Allowing no recourse fate takes our daily lives
Into
Its guarded possession

Love of existence sustained by pride of accomplished deeds
Becomes in death a residual memory
Only

To be finally dispersed in a historical
Face
Of
A generation

Laments striking at long silences in processions
Led
By mourners
Persist over feeble joys
Of
Life's lesser events

For grief never quite finishes adding to
Its
Statue

Sophisticated old and new facades of burial sites
Enhanced by perpetual light

And

A hand of an artist who leaves behind memento
Of
His times

Claim no advantage
Both ancient and modern man pay dues to implacable gods

Mercury

A courier is in care of sealed envelopes
Taking over the fate of vital messages marked
As
Utmost urgent

Rain on his eyelids adds to his fatigue
Seeking its niche twilight sets in into the breathing
Pores
Of high rises

Yet it concerns him not when he dwells upon the letter
Dutifully repeating in his mind directives received
From
A trusting clerk

He finds a temporary safety in Sisyphus like elevators
Chasing
In a mood of perpetuating self pity
After the nebulas of the murky rich skies

For a brief moment he wonders in earnest about matters
Of
Great importance

Someone's life decided already with a binding
Signature

Coming to terms with the fact he would never satisfy a need
To know important detail of the last minute proposal

Without a second thought he rushes out of buildings

Back between colonnades braced with metal and glass

A soldier at home inside the maize of streets swirling with crowd
Emissary of news to the curiosity seeking Olympic gods

On ancient agorae

Rain emulates your sensuality as
It
Gains velocity

Hear a calling of my footprints coming
From
A square of ancient agorae

Let us unearth love suffering and longing of ages
Among
A pile of rubble
Where shells of broken vases extend ceramic necks

Back towards vapours of earth

To overcome inherent weaknesses we must
First
Pay homage to an old illusion

That silence of gods permits our many conquests

Because life will not flourish by itself until we sanctify
Its
Many benefits

Pray with me for permanence of white marble stones at times
When
Iron crypts cave in weakened by tongues of rust

On guard of gothic

Evening celebrates fanciful forms of entertainment
Only candid night brings back time held
By
Clepsydrae

I'm sleepwalking on the grounds of
12th century
Castle

In time to witness armoured knights perform
Duties scheduled by their masters

Despite witnessing death certificates kept
Within possessed by secrecy
Halls of archives
They
Do not sleep idle beneath heavy layers of tombs
Left without grandeur of
A cause

From shadows nestled in medieval stones they
Walk out in groups of seven convinced
By late hours' calling
Of
A need to stand on guard of gothic

On the way to the altar

Days of joy and wonder swayed by a noncompliant hold
Of
Melancholy

We welcome the moment to detach ourselves from issues
Of
No consequence

An esoteric aroma of exotic flowers provokes an obligation
Not
To underestimate our own defencelessness

Grateful for words we dissect stories into fragments easy
To
Comprehend

In hope light of truth will not be lost amidst insurgencies
Of great peril

Holding on to steady hands of angels we visit voting altars
Set up
On the outskirts of city inflamed by prayers

Where a rising hand of god has a will to contain in an instant
The wrath of elements

Passers-by

Well suited to maintain the status of anonymous random
Passers-by

Our presence in the streets is as relevant
As well defined perimeters of repetitive blue shadow
On master's aquarelles

Arrived at
By
His work in solitaire

With a slight effort we bend our shoulders
Forward

To make that first hesitant step before crossing
Busy
Intersections

Although silky thread of light in hour of dawn
Is
Not yet overbearing with assigned to us
Tasks

When sun overtakes a passing drizzle we walk side by side only
To
Break a temporarily formed
Comradeship

By
A sudden change of pace

From a distance we form a nameless crowd changing
Its
Shape as it moves forward to its purpose

Our faces indistinguishable behind a sheet
Of
Falling dusk

Form an impressionistic view of humanity

Rain

Fostering morning dreams rain stops
By
On its way from perishing fast

Kingdoms of night

Arrested on the other side of austere looking
Window panels

Its
Evanescent grace purifies long hours of melancholy

Coming down rooftops eaves rain deliberates
Its
Next musical note

Playing to the delight of earth and to the scrutiny of connoisseurs
Of
Sound

River flow

Acquiescent sea swallows up the longing imbedded
In
Deep currents of relentless river

A man protected by comfort zone
Of
His dwelling
Makes incorrect computer entry

As he pauses to disrupt monotony of engagement
He
Glances
Leisurely around his room

His eyes focus for a brief moment
On
The crossing of light and self-portrait as a young man

Alerted he can refuse no longer a primeval call

He ties himself up to the river's
Permanent flow

Road to nowhere

You followed the road to nowhere
To
Sign in
On a high mountain of dreams

How easy you entrusted yourself to that route
Along
Crawling darkness of bush line behind your every step

Believing it will lead you once again far away
From
Every day matters becoming
Burdensome

But mistaken you were having not taken under consideration
Strained from
Pain
Shoulders

Able they were not to take you further than the next stage
Of
Initiation

That suffering somehow becomes incurable

You have taken your name and possessions with you
Leaving
Me with a landscape moulded by your hands

Of
Life deprived of a right to once joyful beginning

Against the judgment of prophets

Birds find sanctuary in summer leaves under blue shades
Of
A charismatic sky

Your eyes are mystifying light green
With all the secrets
Of
Your thoughts
Open
To free interpretation

Stop pretending we've never met

At times your name appears on my writing pad
Like
An urgent memo

Ready to reinvent itself into a new beginning
Or
To find long awaited excuses

Seldom day without you seems so crestfallen
As
Today
When it's nearing its end

Come back to me with or without an intention
To
Give consent to love endurance

Against the best judgments
Of
Your own prophets

Our first kiss

One day we'll meet in a secluded garden
Folded into shadow

Of
A lenient night

Like old-time lovers we will be free
Of
Fears

The first date so often inflicts

Moon our only strategist will
Gently lead us into each other
Arms

Witnessing our first kiss

Sermon

Waiting for a moment of silence Jesus summons His eloquence
In front
Of
Curiosity seeking crowd

Summer thirst wraps tightly around the throats of onlookers
Eager
To applaud or use derision as a weapon
Of
Their choice

Ever gentle wind plays with teacher's robe
Its
Purple dye
Improvising upon reflection of light
As He moves forward with hands turned outwardly
In
A gesture of disagreement with a status quo

Or
When He is torn between words
He must instantly deliver

There is a moment of pause brought by chaos
Of
Falling stacks of produce

Noise of unruly cattle sold to new owners
Marketplace filled with its own usual
Sounds

Those whose sins are not yet fully acknowledged
Are voicing their opinions
Others
Listen carefully to new decrees as He continues

Placing orders
Upon
Judges' scales and then upon reality

Halfway through the sermon He lifts His eyes toward the sun
Merciless
In
Zenith

Shallow riverbed

Trees are falling recklessly down in time
Of
Disillusionment

Shallow riverbed is my home where I sleep
At
Night in the presence of moon

My days belong to sandy shores of beach and shining attributes
Of
Deliberate sun

If you visit me I will show you a scar where my lungs were cut open
By
A knife

But I have been healed by a word of a wandering magician
Who
Also gave me a talisman

I learned the language of a fish and I came to understand
Why
Birds perfect their flight

Gradually I reclaim a price I've paid for temporary
Arrangements
By
Taking hope for the licence to prevail

My only possession is a mirror framed in silver I found
In
Unclaimed debris
Left behind by someone who did not care anymore

She is blind

She is blind yet she arranges her kingdom
In orderly manner when she steps

Into
A world of squeaking wooden furniture
Metal frames
Glass

Hesitantly touching piece by piece fawning
To her hands

She goes out in the rain and raindrops slide freely down
Her forehead upon her eyelids splashing
On her rejuvenated
Mouth

She goes out in the sun and sun penetrates her young skin until
It catches golden shade changing into amber

When loneliness finds its nest in the folds
Of
Long winter night

She reaches towards the light arched high above darkness
Splitting it into the rainbow of invisible

Snowfall

Snowfall hesitates a clavichord note
If
Only town is asleep

In daylight it opens a pantomime musical
Of
Eyes blinding fantasy

Originated in celestial abodes it knows
No human joy or grievance

Distant and properly detached it allows
No regrets but lets folly of
Hope
Feed minds restored to peace already

Sailing forth in a wake of our desires
We
Are safe to beckon its harmony

Somewhere

Somewhere along a tree line horizon mercilessly slides
Its
Narrow curtain

I become truly entranced retrieving old
Memoirs

Playing hopscotch game with intertwined chains
Of
Accidental events

In order to validate my gains entrenched
In
The past

But deeper into wasteland

Are

Prayers silenced by the needs
Of
Neglected orphans

Scattered birds fleeing disarray
Of
Wilderness

Torment of flowers withering slowly
When
Clouds above are threatening

Strangers

Historically your name dwells in an unsolicited depth
Of
Solitude

Disguised as a rule of law against the first shout of defiance
When you announced your miraculous presence at birth

You hide your face behind the mask of laughing moon
Lured by darkness released from mind
Of
Universe

You will not be portrayed along those
Who
Left earth in an aura of fame
Or
Good fortune

Your address is unknown devoid of a sense of mystery even
To
A mail
Delivery person

Neither next generation gradually impeding to take over control
Of the future emitting new illusions

Nor will I remember how you looked yesterday
When you walked leisurely in the nearby park

You are a stranger I see everyday in the same streets
Of metropolis we call our home

Stream of daylight converges to disperse into elongated shadows
On our paths as we meet in a convention of silence

Alike in our common lives marked by the same memento mori
In close anonymous arrays shoulder to shoulder we depart

Strawberries in her garden

She
Unfolds the day with morning mist
Held
Firmly in her plain hands

Neither weak nor strong
In her convictions
She
Repeats her daily tasks
Stitching loose threads back
Into tightly woven
Patterns

With the corner of her homemaker's
Eyes
She notices
What has been torn by
Use
Or
Neglect
And makes a note of it

She has strawberries in her garden

A tale

It's a night in distress
Not a sound
Of
An owl

Heart of darkness falls upon
Gaping mouths
Of
Silver rivers

A tale of man's life conceals
A lesson
In
Surrender

The one betrayed by autumn

The one betrayed by autumn spends agonizing hours
Pleading
For

A right to a name that was once his identity and belongings
Acquired
In
Toil lost in time of a sudden eclipse of senses

He wonders if he ever had a home having no memory
Of
A recent past

Fallen angels bring to his feet empty baskets braced with
Wreath of dying flowers

Alerted by a growing distrust fearing twilight converging upon
Yellowish in drought blades of grass

He moves forward

All the way to broad boulevards where marble palaces lit
By
Sun revolving violently
Inside the apocalyptic ring of fire

Arise from rubble by the will of giants to fall back into rubble
With a sound of devilish derision

Three Magi

With arid air sustaining everlasting love of desert
Three Magi are well advanced in their journey

Gifts they have chosen in agreement with wisdom
Lay well protected under many folds of rich fabrics

Their eyes slightly raised above never tired camels
See truth as a diversified form of life in continuum

Behind light swirl of sand horizon moves forward
Steadily escaping into the mouth of open space

Distances by now became a matter of free assumptions
Nobody tries to arrive at conclusive estimates of reality

Long silences are filled with soul-searching finality
On account of mirages they are willing to unravel

Not knowing how long it takes to fulfill one's destiny
They move toward white walls enslaved by sunlight

Tired hands

Tired hands will not submerge with ease in overwhelming goodness
Of
Sunshine

Marked with bruises they chiselled names
Of
New heroes on facades of age resilient monuments

Lifted cargo all day at the request of customers
Whose goods had to arrive on schedule

Cleaned streets homes offices of dust debris scattered
In
The back alleys

Paper crumpled in waist baskets

Dug into long corridors of northern arctic mines
Excavated clods of salt from the inhospitable pit

Of
Earth

Tired hands studied carefully turns of life
To know that tomorrow betrays the meek

Therefore

They go on fulfilling duties assigned to them
At new dawn

Able

To
Calm hearts of angry wood copper and stone

To Michael Cloutier

I call it a period of scenery engrossed in drama when leaves fall
Only surface deep
Golden

Before they crash with the vehement force
Of
Wind

Fastened to mysticism by
A blood
Of
Your aboriginal ancestors

You were raising a new house hidden
Between overlapping layers
Of
Past and present autumns

To
Surround them with animated trees

Feeding us a renegade visions
Of
Transformed into nothingness

Rituals

To later redeem every misconception of
Self

When at the crossing of your exorcist
Eyebrows

A sign of nihilistic strain
Marked

A final point of realization that repetitive sacrifices
Meet the fate of mutant forest consumed
By
Fire within

To Michael Nelson

You write your own songs spreading sad news on wings
Of
Black raven

Allow the spirit of returning to you raven
To
Feed your senses
With a remindful voices from wilderness

Because darkness impressed upon you
Harnesses memory of suffering

As
You wrestle with the loss of innocence

While a cradle of night only deepens your sorrow
Taking away from you the last resort of forgiveness

To Ted Harrison

You make us see the sun as you rejoice in it
A bright playful ball suspended
By
The will of your eyes
On canvases bright with willing colours

Small animals
Miniature people engaged in activities at the footsteps

Of
Sky reaching mountains

Outside air looks clear with a breeze

I was a child once entrusted by wise teachers
To
Love of life

As it never stops to flourish on the outskirts of our vision

Taking on fresh appearances even from decaying fossils
Soon overgrown by vibrant sprouts
Of
Foliage
Along roads forcing their way to meet a submissive line
Of
A horizon

Waiting for a hand of an artist to awaken a new despair
For hues perceived seldom represent reality

Trees are giving in to apathy

I search the end of autumn finding no doors in this labyrinth
Of
Slow decay

My feet stumble upon branches
Of
Poplar trees
Unable to stop the bleeding from veins cut open

White necks of birches lay strewn by an evil hand
Under the caving
Of
A bridge

Trying to enhance my home with late blooming
Flowers I fail

To
Recapture spirit of necessity
River over cataracts cautiously leads me towards

The
Only path well chosen for its safety

But within my peripheral vision even century old trees
Have given in to apathy

Ulysses comes home

Ulysses fought many battles in a foreign war
Holding on to victories like a fact
Of
His manhood

He worked as a salesman at Goodwill Co.
Travelling often between small towns
Of
Orange County
Selling small electronic gadgets

It was then
He detected every nuance
Of
A human desire to possess and the price
He was willing to
Pay for own misguided
Pride

He worked as a bartender in a nightclub
Called
StarAlley in Memphis

Liverpool
Or
Hong Kong

But he was too quick to spot a lonely woman
Sitting by herself in an oblivious rowdy crowd

Her
Eyes detached
Betraying some inconsolable loss or perhaps
A trail
Of
Loneliness

He delivered pizza to various addresses in New York
Getting small change for a tip

He drove a bus in the streets of San Francisco
Where he experienced
A brief attachment
To
A city

When he came back to Suzanne they sat down at the table together
She opened Heinz tomato soup

Walk along the beach

Redeemed by early September our steps collect silence
As
We walk side by side

Words betray hastiness in their eagerness
To
Verbalize what feelings are unable to deliver

I elect to remain out of your reach caressing
Blue
Outline of ocean

Find me by means of metaphors in dreams
If
You need

Angel's extraordinary veins in you try
To
Inflict future upon fine grains of sand

Watch carefully the first act of a new drama
Is now unfolding

The last night prayer

You walked upon dusty sunset boulevards with golden sandals
On
Your feet

Surrounded by those who cherish voluntary acts
Of
Miracles

Born in a cradle of inconspicuous deliverance
By
The will of wise prophets

At birth acquiring a privilege to digress with ease
On
Matters of evil and good

You imposed your own set of rules above those whose
Own
Conflicting voices became a cause

Of
Disagreements and confusion

In soul-searching dogmas your sound judgment
Prevailed over the tumult and discord
Of
Competing for bravery and knowledge
Centuries

You acknowledged a need for celebrating
Old
And new rituals
As you prayed at night in olive garden not yet fully aware

Of the price you must pay for passage into history

Who is this man?

Who is this man who blindly follows a narrow trail among indifferent
Blades of grass

In search for a Golden Grail

Who is this man who scatters pebbles from under his feet as he leaves
Behind a sound of joy in a crowd easy to please

With a resolve never to look back at forsaken prizes

Who is this man who reaches down to respectful earth
Lifts a fresh clod of clay to his virgin eyes

In wonder over its origins

Who is this man on a quest to find answers by confronting
His twin image upon surfaces of mirrors

Framed in silence

Who is this man who appears to be naïve in his earnest
Praying for a seed of mercy

At the end of one's sacrifice

Who is this man who beckons voices of wilderness to come
To
His rescue
In a flight from oppressive imprisonment

Of his own consciousness

Who is this man who has nothing to fear from idols erected
At
Crossroads
Yet he implores an honour of man to stand by his side

Over the promise of heaven

Who is this man who knows only the romance of moonlight
Evoking ridicule

Yet he is present in all of us

Your image

Image of your suffering shown on medieval canvases resonates faith
In
Resolve of followers
Engaged in arguments with disbelievers

Time endorsed dogmas preserved on ancient scrolls
Lay hidden protected from acts
Of
Sacrilege

Deciphered by a few only those who have trained themselves
In
Rigours of higher hierarchy

You are faced with reverberating dilemmas
As
We all enter into the next period

Escapism into freedom from bounds of ethics
When a mood of general decline
In
Values marks the onset of a new
Millennium

Brings upon you demands to reinforce merits
Of
Your kingdom based on rewards of heart kindled
By spirit of forgiveness

Regardless of our proneness to failure documented
In archives of humanity

Heavenly trumpets sounded repeatedly words
Of
Judgment

That a fall from grace has become a predicament of man
In
Elaborate scheme of gods

Leaving him limited to sort out laws according to his ability
In
Self-governance

Yet you do not cease in giving continuous testimony
To
Facilitate the rebirth of your tenure

Endorsing
Fabulous ceremonies in service of your praises
Conducted by selected saints

Showing mercy to a mind wrestling with a sin
Lessening the poverty of disillusion

Belated is your knowledge

You leave a string of beads at the foot of voting altar in hope gods
Would not pass them by without taking notice

Belated is your knowledge though unrestrained
In
Its quest to take over all you possess

But you allow yourself not to utter words ascending into definite
Meanings

For fear your senses will loose a battle with a cold heart
Of
Mind in a complete command

In vanity you defy urgency of everyday matters
To
Rejoice for a moment
At the door
To Sesame your reason trapped by shades of gold

You judge approving gains free of harm to others
And postpone the oncoming guilt with an inborn pride

When doubt sets in into late hours of night you ride the ebbing tide
On
The way out to the other shore

When dawn steps in

Silence of night dispersed behind rising from a distance range
Of
Gentle hills

Dawn steps into a valley filled with peaceful
Intentions

Trees towering above river dock appease the eye of onlooker
Its coat
Of
Greenery covered with morning dew

You open a window towards east road where sun emerges
Slowly from behind
Winding curves
Of
Horizon

All of a sudden a chorus of birds begins its
Ceremony of songs at the start of a day

Unsettling surge of fear makes you aware that new hardships
Still await you
And you examine the idyllic scenery with a growing distrust

Yet you have to wonder how easily you walk above each new illusion
Never looking down into the bottom
Of
Precipice
Unaware of its many perils

It's the belief in a sense of duty ironed to your pride by
forefathers
Which is your shield
Against
Moments weakening your spirit

Sometimes you brace yourself with shiny aura of sun sometimes
With
Moonlight
Unable to find consolation in tenets of rightful gods

Praying instead to earth

A new day begins at dawn

A new day begins at dawn pregnant with news
For
Those in waiting

Shouldered by the rim of space doves spread out nimble
Wings
In readiness for the first flight

Awaken from a sleep you are back under the command of mind
Scrupulously measuring time allotted to you by Moira

By a force of will your eyes feed on a morning light
For the right to once again perceive beauty

Earth slowly reveals its shape widening the scope of horizon

In
Your heart
Spring of hope arises

At dusk

Lost in its journey the last ray of sun finds its way
To
A crevice in a rock
Before dusk sets in above the nest of the valley

Following the motion of space fleeing towards distant universe
A rapid creek flows
Straight
Into
The arms of awaiting river

Birds hide in the thickest of leaves
Fearing uncertainty of oncoming night

From a scrub of young beech a late visitor appears
With hands around his lips
He
Summons echo in a loud voice

Beauty escapes

You paint pleasant landscapes using words devoid of sadness
That beauty escapes mind's resourcefulness

Leaving those who attempt to posses its reflection on earth
Empty handed

Well versed by years of patient study in human condition
You
Don't let be swayed by pride
In your needs to verbalize more than permitted by silence

Lest you awake anger of gods whose acts are often cruel

Facing new day

Mountains emerge from the hold of night reclaiming a view
Of the valley covered with transient patches of fog

An old clock on the wall is turning each minute into
An accurate distance away from its past working its way

Like a train

Forward crushing all dreams on a threshold of regained
Consciousness

A man awakens to his duties with a desire to benefit from his effort
Children are born to a world of small and great miracles

Gods are pleased with you

Gods are pleased with you glad to see your compliance in fulfilling
Designated duties

In a matter of fact manner you exercise the right
To
Use resources of life proliferating earth

Finding with ease the only path leading to hidden
In
A bulrush spring

You celebrate summertime becoming a spectator
Of
Sunsets lingering above the promise of horizon

In a belief there must to be a temporary refuge
On the other side of a mountain range

A home to those who like you easily succumb
To a fever of distant constellations

Inside the labyrinth

All of a sudden you are lost surrounded by intricate lay out of labyrinth
With trappings behind every step

A fine thread of silk Ariadne gave to you has been torn in a moment
Of
Inattention
From a distance an inhuman voice demands further sacrifices

In a sudden turn of feelings you reach for a sword making sure
It remains securely fastened to your side

For you just don't know anymore if you are still the one in pursuit
Or
Perhaps
You are now being chased as often is the irony of unforeseen fate

Firebrand in your hand paints archetype shadows splashing dance
Macabre along whitewashed walls of corridors availing no exit

You came here from an oversees country answering the call
Of
Bravery
Placing trust in deceptive ways of man

Minotaur overburden by the weight of solitude begins to lead you
To
His den
Feeling the end of his days has finally arrived

Overcoming weakness of mind at last you deliver a fatal blow
To a welcoming its own demise beast

An ancient tale has ended but since many more have entered
The labyrinth

Birthrights

Moon guards its many secrets behind mournful shield
Of
Clouds

In a séance like dream I explore deep trenches where a chronicle
Of
Time opens page after page

Evidence gathered leads towards conclusion
Of
Existence of yet another civilization

Established by its diligent inhabitants only to perish
In
A moment of general mood of despair or for reasons
Unknown to us

Excavated mouth of earth brings fossils back to its surface
Encoded presence of loose-knitted events
Persists in a collective
Memory
Of
Greatness poisoned by a lasting spell of neglect

Detailed composites of bones pieces of ceramic bowls
Preserved in subsequent stadiums of decay continue to command
Our
Need to meticulously classify
Our
Beginnings

Before our own flesh and spirit will also be discarded along
Ancient riverbank without a claim made
By
Powers higher than humanity

Born into the task of bearing the burden of inherited past
We attain a dissolve from further inquiries
At
An hour of death

When stars in turn reinvent our humble lives
Into
Mind pleasing fables
Adding our names to an old mythology while universe unravels itself

Returns of mornings

Grain of faith mirrors life allowing me to see its daily reoccurrence
Even though I have forsaken the ritual of praying

With a new will day unveils seething with rain trees
Rich in ornaments altars rise up at the crossroads
Entirely devoted
To
Autumn

Lured by a sudden premonition of tomorrow elderly half open Windows
Bringing back the memory of fleeing away river

Knowing by now that time left its credo in the biblical mountain
Soon within the reach

Marble statue

You stand in aura of fame a marble statue indebted to the skillful hand
Of
An artist

Against the final word of death you view the landscape again
This time with eyes carved in a sturdy stone

Time and time again you look back at the past tracing your footprints
Still faithful to your cause

Yet your name included with zest in a book of history
Answers now to its own unpredictable fate

Printed in the United States
33179LVS00013B/3